Teaching Spelling

Through

Writing

Teaching Spelling Through Writing

Patricia J. Hagerty

1994

TEACHER IDEAS PRESS
A Division of
Libraries Unlimited, Inc.
Englewood, Colorado

*To my sister Laurie
and brother Jerry.*

And special thanks to Jennifer Partridge, the fourth-grade teacher without whose help this book would not be possible.

Copyright © 1994 Patricia J. Hagerty
All Rights Reserved
Printed in the United States of America

No part of this publication may be reproduced, stored in a retrieval system, or transmitted, in any form or by any means, electronic, mechanical, photocopying, recording, or otherwise, without the prior written permission of the publisher. An exception is made for individual library media specialists and teachers who may make copies of activity sheets for classroom use in a single school. Other portions of the book (up to 15 pages) may be copied for in-service programs or other educational programs in a single school.

TEACHER IDEAS PRESS
A Division of
Libraries Unlimited, Inc.
P.O. Box 6633
Englewood, CO 80155-6633

Library of Congress Cataloging-in-Publication Data

Hagerty, Patricia J.
   Teaching spelling through writing / Patricia J. Hagerty
  vii, 58 p. 17x25 cm.
  Includes bibliographical references (p. 56).
  ISBN 1-56308-132-6
  1. English language--Orthography and spelling--Study and teaching (Elementary) 2. English language--Composition and exercises--Study and teaching (Elementary) I. Title.
LB1574.H33 1993
372.6'32--dc20   93-30269
                                                                         CIP

Contents

INTRODUCTION vii

1 WHY TEACH SPELLING THROUGH WRITING? 1

   Reasons to Teach Spelling Through Writing 2
      Spelling Is a Process 2
      Spelling Is Not Isolated from Language Use 2
      Spelling Errors Are Not Random 3
      Lack of Transfer to Writing 4
      Instruction Is Based on Individual Needs 5

2 GETTING STARTED: Determining Spelling Needs
   and Forming Spelling Groups 7

   Determining Spelling Needs 7
      Collecting a Writing Sample 7
      Evaluating the Samples 8
      Determining Individual Spelling Needs 10
   Forming Spelling Groups 13
      Forming Spelling Groups Formally 20
      Forming Spelling Groups Informally 20

3 SPELLING MINI-LESSONS: Whole Class Instruction 24

   What Are Mini-Lessons? 24
      Characteristics of Mini-Lessons 25
   Examples of Whole Class Mini-Lessons 26
      Completing a Spelling Log 26
      Proofreading for Spelling 27
      Using Sources 27
      How to Have-a-Go-at-It 28
      Using Standard Spelling and Functional Spelling 28
      Where to Keep Frequently Misspelled Words 28
      Getting Ready for a Spelling Conference 32
      Participating in a "Spelling Explorers Circle" 32
   Modeling Whole Class Mini-Lessons 33
      How to Have-a-Go-at-It 33
      Proofreading for Spelling 34
   Keeping Track of Mini-Lessons 34

4 SPELLING MINI-LESSONS: SMALL GROUP INSTRUCTION 35

   Examples of Small Group Mini-Lessons 35
      Apostrophes in Contractions 35
      Apostrophes to Show Possession 36
      Homophones 36
      Doubling a Final Consonant Before Adding an Ending 37
      Capitalizing Proper Nouns 37
      Correctly Spelling High Frequency Words 37
      Making Plurals from Words Ending in *x, s, sh, ch* 37
      Words Beginning with *kn* and *n* 38
      The Two Sounds of *c*: *k* and *s* 38
      Dropping the *e* Before Adding *ing* 38
   Modeling Small Group Mini-Lessons 39
      Correctly Spelling High Frequency Words 39
      Dropping the *e* Before Adding *ing* 40
   Fitting Small Group Mini-Lessons into the Writing Period 40
   Individual Mini-Lessons 41

5 ASSESSMENT IN A PROGRAM THAT
   TEACHES SPELLING THROUGH WRITING 42

   Teacher Assessment of Student Progress 42
      Edited Drafts 42
      Checklists and Anecdotal Records 43
      Progress Toward Goals 44
   Teacher Assessment of Attitudes 47
   Student Assessment of Progress and Attitudes 49
      Spelling Evaluation Sheets 49
      Looking at Written Work 51
      Progress Toward Goals 51

6 LINGERING QUESTIONS 52

   And in Conclusion... 55

   REFERENCES 56

   ABOUT THE AUTHOR 58

Introduction

During the past decade, increasing numbers of teachers have been examining their beliefs about teaching reading and writing and are implementing process-based approaches. As teachers organize literature-based reading programs and writing workshops, they are beginning to examine how the teaching of spelling fits into these instructional programs. Should spelling continue to be taught through the memorization of words on a weekly list, despite the scarcity of evidence that such a practice leads to better spelling in writing (Parry and Hornsby, 1988; Cochrane 1984)? and that such a program isolates spelling instruction from real writing activities? Should spelling be taught through writing? If so, how?

The purpose of this book is to help practicing classroom teachers in grades two through six learn how to organize and implement a program in which spelling is taught through writing. After discussing why teaching spelling through writing is important, the book will help teachers learn how to determine their students' spelling needs; form spelling groups; give whole class, small group, and individual mini-lessons; and evaluate student progress.

Teaching Spelling Through Writing is targeted primarily for teachers in grades two through six because most students are not ready for a formal spelling program until the middle of second grade, when they are deep into the transitional stage of spelling. Children in kindergarten, first grade, and the beginning of second grade are going through stages of spelling development (Gentry, 1987). As they go through the precommunicative, semiphonetic, phonetic, and transitional stages on their way to "correct" spelling, they should be free to work on communicating ideas and building fluency. They also should be receiving informal instruction and feedback about the way words are spelled through writing conferences.

Teachers in grades seven and above should be able to adapt the content of this book to their own curricula and teaching situations.

1

Why Teach Spelling Through Writing?

The decisions we make about the teaching of spelling usually reflect our views of spelling and spelling instruction. Consider your beliefs about the following questions:

- Is spelling a *process* of predicting, confirming, and integrating, or is it a *product* arrived at by the memorization of a list of words?

- Should spelling be learned in isolation, or should it be integrated with writing and reading instruction?

- Do children make careless mistakes with their spelling, or do spelling errors follow a predictable pattern?

- Do you observe children correctly transferring to their writing the spelling of words memorized from a list, or do they seem to misspell the memorized words as well as high frequency words when involved in daily writing experiences?

- Should spelling instruction be based on individual needs, or should all students receive instruction on the same words?

- Should students view spelling as a list of words to be memorized, or should they regard it as something that is important to writing?

- Should parents continue to view spelling as a list of words to be memorized, or can they be led to understand that the most important thing about spelling is that words are correctly spelled in writing, especially final drafts?

How you answer these questions provides insight into your philosophy about spelling and probably into how you teach it. If you understand that spelling is a process, that spelling instruction should be integrated with writing and reading, and that spelling errors are not random, then you need to do more than give students a weekly list to memorize. If you have observed that children do not necessarily spell the words learned from a list correctly in authentic writing experiences, believe that spelling instruction should be based on individual needs, and feel that both children's and parents' views of spelling need to change, then teaching spelling through writing seems a more logical approach.

Reasons to Teach Spelling Through Writing

Spelling Is a Process

In the past, many educators taught reading and writing as an accumulation of a set of skills. If children learned to recognize short vowels, long vowels, punctuation, and so on, then they would be readers and writers. Reading and writing was a matter of applying those skills to print. Now, many teachers view both reading and writing as processes. When looking at reading as a process, we know that readers make predictions that guide their reading, confirm these predictions as they read by asking if what they are reading makes sense and "sounds like language," and integrate information as they interact with text (Goodman, 1980). In the writing process, we know that writers think about their ideas, get them down, and continue to work with them as they put pen to paper (Calkins, 1986).

Just as our views of reading and writing have changed, so have our views of spelling instruction. Spelling is much more than the accumulated knowledge of a set of words. It is a process that involves predicting the order in which we think the letters will go based on phonics (letter/sound relationships), orthographics (the ways letters are grouped into words), or sight (our memories of what the word looks like).

We continue the process as we write the word, confirming that the spelling is correct or incorrect. We often do so by asking ourselves if the word we are spelling "looks right." If it doesn't look right, we may try to write it several ways until it does. We then integrate the spelling of the word into our storehouse of knowledge. This word may not at first be integrated correctly, but with continued exposure to the word through reading and writing and/or through instruction, we eventually learn the correct spelling. This spelling process closely parallels the reading process of predicting, confirming, and integrating.

Spelling Is Not Isolated from Language Use

Spelling is very much a part of reading, writing, speaking, and listening (Buchanan, 1989). As children read and listen, they gain knowledge of words, their usage, and underlying concepts, leading to improvement in oral and written expression. While reading, children gain a sense of how a word should look, which helps them in attempts to spell. When they write, they learn about spelling patterns, phonics, and meaning relationships among words. For example, they may notice that *took* is much like *book*. This information helps them as spellers, listeners, and readers (Cochrane, 1984).

When children are only exposed to lists of words for spelling instruction, they see spelling as a separate subject having little to do with writing. They think of spelling as nothing more than the memorization of words, and they think they are good spellers if they get a high grade on a spelling test, regardless of how they spell words in written work (Hagerty and Partridge, 1991).

Spelling instruction is more meaningful to children if it is integrated into reading and writing instruction (Routman, 1991). Then they see spelling as a meaningful part of writing and realize its importance in conveying their message. As a student named Amanda said, "If you don't spell words correctly in your writing, the person trying to read it won't know what you're trying to say."

Children realize that they learn a lot about spelling by reading, because the words they see are the ones they will be likely to use when writing (Hagerty and Partridge, 1991). When spelling is taught through the writing process, children begin to see the interrelatedness of the tools needed for communication.

Spelling Errors Are Not Random

The spelling errors that children make reflect their understanding of letter-sound correspondence and reveal stages of spelling development (Gentry, 1982; Buchanan, 1989; Wilde, 1992). Briefly, according to Gentry (1982), these stages include:

1. Precommunicative

    Spelling consists of a random stringing together of letters and numbers (*nstr* may be the spelling for *house*).

2. Semi-phonetic

    Some letter-sound associations are present. The child is just beginning to learn that letters represent sounds (*kt* may be the spelling for *cat*).

3. Phonetic

    Every sound feature of a word that a child hears is represented in the word (*prsn* may be the spelling for *person*).

4. Transitional

    The child begins to rely more on sight than sound for spelling. More conventions of spelling are noticeable. The correct letters of a word may be included, but in the wrong order. Many words are correctly spelled (*nihgt* may be the spelling for *night*).

5. Correct

    At this stage, the child has a good grasp of the spelling rules of the English language. Most words are correctly spelled.

It is important to note that these stages are fluid; children do not move concretely from one stage to the next. With continuous writing and reading experience and feedback from those around them, they move gradually through the stages, exhibiting characteristics of more than one stage at a time.

Children spell words incorrectly because they often have not yet internalized a spelling generalization or pattern or have not had enough experience with reading and writing. In a program in which spelling is taught through writing, spelling errors can be analyzed to determine needs, and mini-lessons (discussed in Chapter 3) can be used to convey the knowledge children need to become better spellers.

We also need to realize that children do not learn to spell overnight. Even when they have gone through the stages of spelling development to the "correct" stage, they will continue to misspell words now and then. In fact, we all use two kinds of spelling: standard and functional (Buchanan, 1989). You probably correctly spell most words you write, but you also occasionally use functional spelling. Think of the list you make for grocery shopping. More than likely it will have a word with functional spelling: *veg* for *vegetable, bk pwdr* for *baking powder, yogrt* for *yogurt*, and so on. Do you ever spell *night* as *nite, through* as *thru*? These are all examples of how we use functional spelling; we spell the word in a way that makes sense to us at the time. We are probably aware that it is not the correct spelling, but for our purposes it is acceptable.

Teaching spelling through writing recognizes both kinds of spelling and helps children decide when each is appropriate. When a group of fourth-graders was asked if they should always spell every word correctly in their writing, Matt said, "No. If you know how, you should spell a word correctly. If you don't know how, write something, [and] keep going to get your ideas down." In answer to the same question, Cara said, "No. You have to learn from your mistakes" (Hagerty and Partridge, 1991). These children are learning that good writers use both kinds of spelling.

Lack of Transfer to Writing

One of the most important reasons to teach spelling through writing was mentioned above: many students who are taught spelling through lists do not necessarily transfer the correct spelling of the words they have memorized to their own writing (Parry and Hornsby, 1988; Wilde, 1990). Few need a research study to confirm this problem; we all can give examples of child after child who got 100 percent on a spelling test, only to misspell some of the words in written work the same day. We more than likely did the same when we were in school! When children have lists, they tend to focus on the words as separate entities rather than learning strategies that will carry them across many words. This tendency might be a clue to us that the memorization of words is an exercise in futility, especially if the words are not used frequently by children.

Instruction Is Based on Individual Needs

In a program in which spelling is taught through writing, instruction for each child can easily be individualized. Teachers can analyze misspellings in written work to determine each child's specific spelling needs and use this analysis as the basis for spelling instruction rather than giving all children in the class the same list of words. After the misspellings are identified, children are instructed, usually in small groups, according to their identified needs.

Children's Views of Spelling Need to Change

If spelling is taught through writing, children's views of spelling can change. In a study completed in a fourth-grade classroom in a suburban school district near Denver, Colorado, children who were in a program in which spelling was taught through writing no longer considered spelling as a list of words to be memorized. Rather, they viewed it as something important to writing (Hagerty and Partridge, 1991). As Becky said, "Spelling is important if you want others to read your writing and understand what you say." Cisco noted, "If you are writing a letter to someone and if there is a word spelled wrong, the person might not get the message."

Students did not, however, become overly concerned about spelling in their written work. Jeff noted, "when you write, you have to get your ideas down. Spelling words right if you know how helps you get your ideas out faster." These students' thinking reflected their beliefs that spelling is important to written work.

Parents' Views of Spelling Need to Change

Many teachers give students a list of words to memorize because they feel parents expect it. It is up to us to help parents understand that children will learn to spell just as many words if their instruction is based on individual needs and if they read and write frequently. As they begin to see their children's spelling improve in written work, parents will become supporters of this type of instruction. In the study mentioned previously (Hagerty and Partridge, 1991), parents were generally supportive of the change to teaching spelling through writing, but they had to be informed of how their children would receive spelling instruction. Many commented on their children's improved spelling in written work, and not one challenged the spelling grade on the report card.

In the final chapter of this book, suggestions will be given for how to explain your program to parents.

The reasons discussed above (spelling is a developmental process that is closely related to reading and writing, children often memorize words for tests and misspell them in their writing, and children's and parents' views of spelling can be changed) all help us understand why teaching spelling through writing has merits for children, teachers, and parents. The next chapter will examine how to get such a program started.

2

Getting Started: Determining Spelling Needs and Forming Spelling Groups

There is no one way to teach spelling through writing. Buchanan (1989), Bean and Bouffler (1987), Routman (1991), and Wilde (1992) describe methods that can be adapted to your style of teaching and the needs of your students. The method described here was developed and implemented by a university professor and fourth-grade teacher and has been successfully used for several years. It entails the following steps: collecting a writing sample from each student; analyzing the samples to determine general patterns of spelling errors; and forming groups for instruction based on the patterns shown by each student. It, too, can be adapted to your style of teaching and your own students' needs.

Determining Spelling Needs

This section will address the steps involved in assessing spelling needs. Begin by collecting a writing sample from each student; then evaluate the samples and determine individual spelling needs.

Collecting a Writing Sample

To start the process, ask your students to write a personal narrative on the topic of their choice. You should make this assignment at the beginning of the school year or at the beginning of each quarter or grading period. The students should write about something they know a lot about, care about, and are interested in; it should also be something that is true (Calkins, 1986). A few might ask you to let them write fiction. It's up to you to decide, but ideas seem to flow better for many children when they write personal narrative. You may find it helpful to use the following guidelines:

- Give them as much time as they need to complete the writing.
- Ask them to check it over for spelling. If they think they have misspelled a word, they should circle it and write what they

8 / Getting Started

think might be the correct spelling of the word above the misspelled word.

- Let them use any source they want to find the correct spelling of words while they write and as they check their spelling.

- Do not tell students that this writing sample is the basis for spelling instruction, because they may be more reluctant to take risks.

As the students write, observe their behavior. Do they circle words they think are misspelled? Do they make any attempt to correct misspelled words? If so, what sources do they use? Dictionary? Other books? Friends? Do they write a misspelled word several different ways to see if one version looks right?

Make notes as you observe. What you notice may serve as the basis for mini-lessons when you begin the program. For example, if most of the students are not using the "have-a-go-at-it" strategy, where they write a difficult word several different ways to see if one looks right (Parry and Hornsby, 1988), you can teach this technique in one of your first mini-lessons. In another mini-lesson, you can teach them to circle words they think are misspelled. As you read each of the samples, note the total number of words the student wrote and the number of words spelled correctly and incorrectly. With this count, you can immediately determine who is correctly spelling a high percentage of words. You might also want to compare the number of words written and spelled correctly on the first sample with a later sample in order to find out which students take risks in their spelling.

Evaluating the Samples

After collecting the samples, look through them to find common patterns of spelling errors. As you notice the patterns, jot them down. For example, with a group of third- or fourth-graders, you may notice that certain students have problems with the apostrophes in possessives—some may not use the apostrophe in the correct place, and some may not use it at all. Other students may have difficulty changing endings of certain words before suffixes are added, such as dropping the *e* or doubling a final consonant before adding an ending. Some may misspell basic high frequency words.

Figure 2.1 shows a list of twelve common spelling errors found in one fourth-grade classroom at the beginning of the school year.

It is important to note that these error patterns are particular to one class of fourth-graders at one point in time. Another class may have error patterns that vary from these. The categories (phonics-based errors, meaning-based errors, mechanical errors, inaccurate visual perception, and handwriting) were decided upon by trial and error and after careful examination of the categories in Buchanan's

—Text continues on page 10

Phonics-based errors	1.	Incorrect phonic clues (using wrong letters for a sound)
Meaning-based errors	2.	Possessives a. incorrect placement of apostrophe b. lack of use of apostrophe
	3.	Incorrect use of homophones
	4.	Incorrect spelling of plurals
	5.	Prefix/suffix a. misspelled b. incorrect use of
	6.	Pronunciation error/dialect
	7.	Contractions a. lack of apostrophe b. incorrect placement of apostrophe c. extra letter in contraction/letter omitted d. adding an apostrophe to a word that isn't a contraction
Mechanical errors	8.	Proper nouns not capitalized
	9.	Spaces between parts of compound words/not inserting a space between words (icecream)
Inaccurate visual perception	10.	Right letters, wrong order; letter omitted or added, including silent letter
	11.	Misspelling of a high frequency word
Handwriting	12.	Spelling error due to incorrect cursive letter formation

Note: A spelling error can be coded in more than one category.

Fig. 2.1. Common Spelling Errors—Intermediate Level

Spelling for Whole Language Classrooms (1989). Dividing the spelling error patterns into categories is certainly optional.

A list of common spelling error patterns at the second-grade level might include:

- not dropping the *e* before adding *ing*;

- misspelling the *ay* sound at the end of a word (*plae* for *play*);

- misspelling high frequency words: *by, was, then, because, went*, and so on;

- lack of apostrophe in contractions;

- lack of silent *e* at the end of words (*tak* for *take*);

- spelling *ing* as *en* (*walken* for *walking*);

- starting words with *n* that begin with *kn*;

- misspelling homonyms: *to, too, two; there, their*.

Determining Individual Spelling Needs

Now that you have a sense of the general spelling error patterns of the whole class, you can begin to focus on each student's individual needs. You might use a spelling evaluation form such as the one shown in figure 2.2 (pages 11 and 12).

It enables you to do the following:

- note the total number of words in the student's writing sample and the percent spelled correctly and incorrectly;

- list each misspelled word, its correct spelling, and the type of error it involves (the type will come from the list of error patterns you developed as you went through the samples the first time);

- summarize the types of errors;

- list what the student does know about spelling; and

- note some general plans for teaching this student.

The last three items are completed on page two of the form. Note that the summary of errors section in figure 2.2 has twelve numbers. These correspond to the number of spelling error patterns listed in figure 2.1. Your summary of errors section may have more or fewer

—Text continues on page 13

Name_____

Total number of words_____ % correct____ % invented_____

# of times misspelling occurs	misspelled word	correct spelling	category of error

Fig. 2.2. Spelling Evaluation Form

12 / Getting Started

Name_____

Summary of Errors

1__   2a__   6__   8__   10__   12__
        b__   7a__   9__   11__
                b__
                c__
                d__
        3__
        4__
        5a__
        b__

What does this student know about spelling?

Teaching plans

Additional comments

Fig. 2.2. Spelling Evaluation Form—*continued*

numbers, depending on the number of common spelling errors you find for your class.

Examining Matt's Writing Sample

The sample shown in figures 2.3 (page 14) was written by Matt, a fourth-grade student.

By looking at Matt's writing sample, the spelling evaluation form might be completed as in figure 2.4 (pages 15 and 16).

Matt, a fourth-grader, has written eighty-seven words in this sample, spelling 83 percent of the words correctly. His spelling error patterns reveal that he needs help with apostrophes for possession and with homophones, specifically *their/there*. He also needs to be reminded that proper nouns start with capital letters and to learn to use the have-a-go-at-it strategy to figure out the spelling of words.

Matt correctly spells many high frequency words (*lots, said, went, there,* and *was,* etc.), and he has some sense of knowing when words are misspelled; in this sample, he circled seven of fourteen misspelled words. (The others were circled by the teacher when she analyzed his sample.)

Examining Brandon's Writing Sample

The sample in figure 2.5 (page 17), completed by Brandon, a fourth-grade student, is different. He wrote eighty-four words and spelled 85 percent of them correctly. By completing the spelling evaluation form (fig 2.6 on pages 18 and 19), it can be seen that he needs help with homophones, specifically *peace/piece* and *to/too*. He also needs help with basic high frequency words such as *said, where, they,* and *any*. Brandon needs instruction in spelling compound words (notice that he often makes them into separate words), and he will need to be reminded to use periods at the end of his sentences and to circle words he thinks might be misspelled. (On this sample, all misspelled words appear to be circled. Brandon only circled one; the rest were done by the teacher as she analyzed the sample.)

Brandon does know the spelling of many high frequency words. He may understand the concept of dropping the *e* before adding an ending (*riding*), and he can correctly spell some contractions (*don't*).

Forming Spelling Groups

There are two general ways to form spelling groups: formally, using the charts provided here, or informally. It is suggested that you start your program using the formal method and then move on to the less formal method when you feel more comfortable determining spelling error patterns. Both approaches will be described in this section.

—Text continues on page 20

Matt A.
Sept. 20, 1990
Mrs. Partridge

Oo One day we went to califonya and spent 3 weeks there. We got to see everythang there. We stayed at my ounts house. There dogs name is boo. My mom boughtᵒᵏ us rist bonds. Mine said 49ers on the top. We had lots of fun. We rode the troly all day. We went to a museum (muesmu) and had lots of fun there. We went to see my cousnis Grad Graguwashon (Graguashon), It was boring. I played tetrus (tetrues) on there canputer. That was fun. I hope we go next year.

Fig. 2.3. Matt's Writing Sample   p 7

Name Matt A.   Sept. 20, 1990

Total number of words 87   % correct 87 % invented 17

# of times misspelling occurs	misspelled word	correct spelling	category of error
1	Califonya	California	8, 1
1	everythang	everything	1, 6
1	aunts	aunt's	2b
11	There	Their	3
1	dogs	dog's	2b
1	boo	Boo	8
1	rist	Wrist	1
1	troly	trolly	10
1	muesma	museum	10
1	Cousnis	Cousins	10
1	Graguashon	Graduation	1, 6 (tion)
1	tetrues	Tetrus	8, 10
1	Canputer	Computer	6

Fig. 2.4. Spelling Evaluation Form Completed for Matt

16 / Getting Started

Name __Matt A.__

Summary of Errors

1 _4_   2a __   6 _3_   8 __   10 _4_   12 __
      b _2_   7a __   9 __   11 __
             b __
             c __
             d __

3 _2_
4 __
5a __
  b __

What does this student know about spelling?

Spells many high frequency words: lots
Knows when words are misspelled   Said
                                                                went
                                                               There
                                                               and

Teaching plans
                                                               was

apostrophes for possession
homophones: their/there
Capitalize proper nouns
Use "have-a-go-at-it"

Additional comments

Fig. 2.4. Spelling Evaluation Form Completed for Matt—_continued_

Brandon L.
Sept. 20 1990
Mrs. Partridge

One day when was out riding my bike when I felt something hit me I looked down it was a peace of hall about pea size to. So then I felt a cupel more hit I groped (cropped) my bike and ran inside. I told my Dad and he siad I hope the don't get big. But thay did we ran down stairs were thay was not eney windows. about an half an later we went up stairs and all exsept one window was broken 8'4" The End.

Fig. 2.5. Brandon's Writing Sample

18 / Getting Started

Name Brandon L.   Sept. 20, 1990

Total number of words 84   % correct 87 % invented 13

# of times misspelling occurs	misspelled word	correct spelling	category of error
1	peace	piece	3
1	hall	hail	1
1	to	too	3
1	cupel	couple	10
1	cropted	grabbed	1
1	siad	said	10, 11
11	thay	they	11
1	were	where	11
1	eney	any	11
1	exsept	except	10
1	up stairs	upstairs	9
1	down stairs	downstairs	9

Fig. 2.6. Spelling Evaluation Form Completed for Brandon

Name Brandon L.

Summary of Errors

1 __2__   2a __   6 __   8 __   10 __3__   12 __
         b __   7a __ 9 __2__ 11 __4__
                 b __
                 c __
                 d __
         3 __2__
         4 __
         5a __
         b __

What does this student know about spelling?

Spells some high frequency words right:
drops e before adding ing (riding)   was
Knows when words are   when
  misspelled   one
                                         something
                                         inside

Teaching plans

homophones: peace/piece   to/too
basic high frequency words: said
Use capital letters at   where
  beginning of sentence   They
have-a-go-at-it   any

Additional comments

Nice printing

Fig. 2.6. Spelling Evaluation Form Completed for Brandon—*continued*

Forming Spelling Groups Formally

By looking over these forms, you can begin to see how to group students for instruction. You can place Matt and Brandon with students who need help with apostrophes for possession. They can also be matched with other students who need help with homonyms. To make this process visually easier, you can use a "whole class needs" sheet to help you group students by need (fig. 2.7). By completing this chart, as was done for Brandon's and Matt's needs (fig. 2.8), you can see at a glance which students make the same types of misspellings and call them together for small group instruction. The numbers across the top of the chart represent the types of spelling error patterns found and listed in figure 2.1. For example, "1" refers to "incorrect phonic clues." Your chart may have less or more numbers, depending on the number of spelling error patterns you found.

These groups should be considered fluid. Writing samples are a good way to form groups to start off your program, but your observations of students' daily written work should provide a great deal of additional information. You will want to create new groups, delete others, or move students to and from groups based on what you notice about their spelling in everyday writing activities.

Forming Spelling Groups Informally

After the first or second go-around of formally evaluating your students' patterns of spelling errors, you should be able to move on to less formal assessments. Once you collect the writing samples, go through them, write the types of errors you notice on a sheet of notebook paper, and jot down the names of the students who demonstrate each particular type of error. For example, if your students show problems with the placement (or lack of placement) of the apostrophes in possessives, the use of homophones, the formation of contractions, the addition of certain suffixes, the inclusion of silent letters in words, or the spelling of basic high frequency words, your sheet may look similar to table 2.1 (page 23).

Using this procedure, spelling groups can be formed quite quickly and with much less paperwork than the formal method requires. However, it takes practice to be able to scan the writing samples and determine patterns of spelling errors. The more formal method may provide the practice you need to move on to evaluating informally.

Date_____

Student	1	2a	2b	3	4	5a	5b	6	7a	7b	7c	7d	8	9	10	11	12

Fig. 2.7. "Whole Class Needs" Sheet

22 / Getting Started

Date_____

Student	1	2a	2b	3	4	5a	5b	6	7a	7b	7c	7d	8	9	10	11	12
Brandon L.	✓			✓										✓	✓	✓	
Matt A.	✓		✓	✓				✓							✓		

Fig. 2.8. "Whole Class Needs" Sheet with Brandon's and Matt's Needs Listed

Misuse/nonuse of apostrophes in possessives

Matt
Christy
Sara

Incorrect spelling of homophones

Matt
Brandon
Riley

Formation of compounds

Tia   Brandon
James
Justin

Adding suffixes

Conor
Tara
Becca

Failure to note silent letters in words

Susie   Jake
Julie   Clark
Evan

High frequency words

Addelle   Bobby
Charlie   Sara
Brandon   Jacob

Table 2.1.

3

Spelling Mini-lessons: Whole Class Instruction

When teaching spelling as described in this book, the teacher collects writing samples, analyzes them to determine spelling patterns, groups students for instruction according to their needs, and uses mini-lessons to teach spelling during writing periods. This chapter will explain what mini-lessons are and where they fit into the writing period. It will also describe some whole class mini-lessons and model how you might use them in your own teaching.

What Are Mini-Lessons?

Mini-lessons are used in process-based classrooms to teach students something they need to know to get better at reading, writing, and spelling. Mini-lessons usually come at the beginning of the reading or writing time and may be taught to the whole class or to a small group.

There are several kinds of mini-lessons (Atwell, 1987). Procedural mini-lessons are oriented to the routines followed during the reading and writing periods, such as where to put folders, where to sit for a peer conference, or how to gather for mini-lessons. Literary mini-lessons teach something related to the writer's craft, such as using good leads, descriptive words, or strong verbs. Strategies/skills mini-lessons may have to do with form in writing (punctuation, paragraphing, spelling), working with unknown words, or choosing appropriate books when reading.

After the mini-lessons, students begin to work on their writing or reading. As they work, they confer with teachers and with each other. The period may end with a share session, where students discuss their reading and/or writing with classmates.

Characteristics of Mini-Lessons

Before describing specific spelling mini-lessons and modeling how you might teach one in your classroom, it is important to note some of their characteristics (Hagerty, 1992).

- Mini-lessons should come from the needs of the students. You should not count on a curriculum guide to tell you what students need. As you observe them and their writing, notice what specific aspects of spelling the students need to get better at. What kinds of things do you need to teach them?

- Mini-lessons are short. You should try to keep them to five to ten minutes. Once you have gone beyond ten minutes, they become what are known as "maxi-lessons." If you know a lesson will be a "maxi-lesson," tell the students in advance. Maxi-lessons, however, should be used sparingly.

- Mini-lessons focus on one thing. Don't try to teach more than one thing in a mini-lesson, because you'll soon lose your students. For example, teach how to circle misspelled words during a mini-lesson but not how to circle misspelled words *and* how to get ready for a spelling conference. Keep in mind, too, that mini-lessons will often have to be taught more than one time. When was the last time you taught your class something once and everyone understood it? Take your cues from your students. If you—and they—don't feel that the lesson was understood, plan to teach it again, maybe even the next day.

- Mini-lessons are purposeful. A spelling mini-lesson should teach the students something concrete to help them improve their spelling, such as dropping the *e* before using *ing*. Other examples of purposeful whole class spelling mini-lessons will be explained later in this chapter.

- Mini-lessons add to class knowledge. What is taught may not be demonstrated by each student right away. Some students may draw on that knowledge that day, whereas others may draw on it days, even weeks, later.

- Use literature as much as you can to teach your mini-lessons. For example, if you want to show students how an *e* is dropped before an ending is added, gather examples of words that follow this pattern from literature the students are reading.

- Mini-lessons end with a connection. You need to help the students apply what they have learned in the mini-lesson to their own writing. For example, if you are modeling the have-a-go-at-it strategy, you might end your mini-lesson with, "So today, when you are writing a word and you aren't sure how to spell it, try to have-a-go-at-it. Write it several different ways to see if one looks right." In the section of this chapter where mini-lessons are modeled, look for the connection at the end of each lesson.

There are excellent sources for learning more about mini-lessons and their roles in Readers' and Writers' Workshops and spelling instruction. Among them are *The Art of Teaching Writing* (Calkins, 1986), *Write On: A Conference Approach to Writing* (Parry and Hornsby, 1988), *Classroom Strategies That Work* (Nathan et al., 1989), *Read On: A Conference Approach to Reading* (Hornsby et al., 1986), *Readers' Workshop: Real Reading* (Hagerty, 1992), *You Kan Red This!* (Wilde, 1992), and *Invitations* (Routman, 1991).

Examples of Whole Class Mini-Lessons

While evaluating the writing samples and noticing spelling error patterns, you will recognize certain general principles and information that all the students could benefit from learning. These can be taught once or twice a week through whole class mini-lessons at the beginning of your writing period (assuming you are writing every day). What students need in whole class mini-lessons would vary from class to class. The mini-lessons described below are only examples, not lessons that you must be sure to teach. Observe and consult with your students to see what *they* need.

Completing a Spelling Log

Using these logs (Parry and Hornsby, 1988), students write a misspelled word from their writing, the correct way to spell the word, and a way to remember its correct spelling. The examples table 3.1 were selected from fourth-grade students' spelling logs:

How I spelled the word	**How it should be spelled**	**How I'm going to remember how to spell it**
becuz	because	I have *a use* for spelling because correctly
famly	family	*I* am in my family
preants	presents	presents might be *sent* to you
siad	said	the word *said* is an *aid* to the speaker

Table 3.1.

With spelling logs, be sure to help the students understand that the device they come up with for remembering the correct spelling of the word must include the part of the word that has been misspelled. Otherwise you may get responses such as these collected from fourth-graders (table 3.2).

How I spelled the word	How it should be spelled	How I'm going to remember how to spell it
frist	first	*frist* not *first*
seakend	second	I play second base.
whan	when	change *at* in *what* to *en*

Table 3.2.

These students are probably not going to learn how to correctly spell these words based on their ideas to help them remember the proper spelling, because they did not focus on the part of the word that was misspelled.

Modeling how to use the logs is extremely important if you want your students' responses to be more like the first examples. They may need direct help to determine how they will remember the spelling of the word. Peer groups are helpful for this activity.

How often should students write in their logs? That is up to you and your students. You might consider asking them to choose two to three words per week from their writing to enter into their logs. Of course, you will have to give the students time to do so and remind them to do it. Ideally, you can work to the point where students will complete the logs on an as-needed basis.

Proofreading for Spelling

An excellent whole class mini-lesson is teaching students how to proofread their work for spelling. When proofreading, students need to start at the end of their piece and work backwards from the last word to the first word. They need to skim the piece, briefly glancing at each word to see if it "looks right." If they think it is misspelled, they should circle it and continue until they have looked at every word. You can ask the students to correct a certain number of the errors by writing the proper spelling above the misspelled word.

Using Sources

Somewhere in your room, set up a table where you and the students can gather resources for use in spelling. Items to consider include a dictionary, a thesaurus, a daily newspaper, a baby-name book, magazines, *The Quick-Word Handbook for Everyday Writers*

(Sitton and Forest, 1987), maps, an atlas, and a hand-held spelling computer. During a mini-lesson, explain the purpose of the resources and give examples of how each can be used. Point out that often the words we want to know how to spell are all around us in print.

In one fourth-grade classroom, students consulted the sports page of the newspaper to find the name of a popular professional football player. Another student used the want ads section to find the correct spelling of "German Shepherd," which she had misspelled on a rough draft.

How to Have-a-Go-at-It

Having-a-go-at-it (Parry and Hornsby, 1988) is merely writing a misspelled word several ways until it "looks right." Students can have-a-go-at-it while writing or during the proofreading stage. They can write the word several different ways in the margin of their paper or on a have-a-go chart (see figure 3.1). The charts shown in figures 3.2 and 3.3 (pages 30 and 31) were completed by second- and fifth-graders. After students try to write the word several different ways, they can ask a parent, their teacher, or another student to write it correctly or they may look it up in the dictionary. The words, correctly spelled in the right-hand column, can be added to individual spelling dictionaries.

In some samples collected from a fourth-grade classroom, one student wrote *sinse, sence,* and *since* before deciding that the latter was the correct spelling. Another student wrote *grate* and *greta* before changing the spelling to *great* on her paper.

Using Standard Spelling and Functional Spelling

As Buchanan mentions in *Spelling for Whole Language Classrooms* (1989), students need to know that there are two kinds of spelling, standard and functional, and they should be allowed to use both in their writing.

In a mini-lesson, you can ask students when they think each kind of spelling is important. Make a list of these reasons and go over them. It is important to help students understand that functional spelling is fine on rough drafts, but that on final drafts standard spelling is the norm. You might want to encourage students to circle words they know are spelled functionally so they can check them later by using resources, asking others, or having a-go-at-it.

Where to Keep Frequently Misspelled Words

This mini-lesson would be considered a procedural one because it helps with the procedure involved with spelling instruction. In this mini-lesson you want to teach students where to record words they

—Text continues on page 32

Name_____

word from my writing	first try	second try	correct spelling

Fig. 3.1. Have-a-Go-at-It Chart

30 / Spelling Mini-Lessons: Whole Class Instruction

Name CONOR

word from my writing	first try	second try	correct spelling
Plaven	Plane	Playing	Playing
Sas	Sayed	S a Y S	Says
toch	toe ch	thich	touch
thes	that	thuts	that's
wils	Rols	R o L es	rules

Fig. 3.2. Have-a-Go-at-It Chart

Name **Brendan**

word from my writing	first try	second try	correct spelling
possibal	posibail	possible	possible
dosent	doesent	doesn't	doesn't
beacauss	because		because
orgerniz	oregenize	oregeinze	organize
wrighting	writing		writing

Fig. 3.3. Have-a-Go-at-It Chart

misspell frequently. The more they see the words they frequently misspell, the more quickly they will learn them. You can ask students to write the correct spelling of words they have trouble with on a 3-x-5-inch card. Have them tape this card to the top corner of their desk and refer to it whenever they need to spell one of those particular words.

Students can also put these words on the "snare board" (Parry and Hornsby, 1988). Provide pieces of construction paper approximately 4-x-8 inches in size. Students can write words that "snare" them—i.e., are troublesome to them—on these pieces of paper. The pieces are put on a bulletin board in the classroom. Students should tell the rest of the class how this word "snares" them.

Students can also keep lists of words that are particularly hard for them in a list on the inside of their spelling folders. Once they believe they have memorized the spelling of the word, they can cross it off. The number of words on the list is up to you and each student. Some students will have more than others.

Getting Ready for a Spelling Conference

It is the student's responsibility to be ready for a spelling conference, which is usually a part of a writing conference. "Being ready" may include being able to show evidence of having applied some of the mini-lessons by updating a spelling log, using the have-a-go-at-it strategy, circling misspelled words, or using sources to find the correct spelling of a word.

Probably the best way to teach this mini-lesson is to model, with a student, how to have a spelling conference. During the modeling, show how you would begin the conference, conduct it, and end it. It is important to note that this type of mini-lesson would probably not be given until each of the strategies (spelling log, have-a-go-at-it, proofreading, using sources) has been modeled in a mini-lesson and students have had opportunities to work with each. You may want to let the students sign up for a spelling conference or make a chart that lists when each individual will be expected to be ready for one. However you decide to do this, make sure you see all students routinely.

Most spelling conferences are held individually, but some may be with small groups. It all depends on how you want to organize your time.

Participating in a "Spelling Explorers Circle"

Another mini-lesson could teach the students how to participate in a "Spelling Explorers Circle" as described in *Whole Language: Getting Started. . .Moving Forward* (Crafton, 1991). This activity gives the students an opportunity to bring troublesome spelling words to a group for help. Students get together in small groups of three or four, and each brings a misspelled word to the group. Using a chart much like the one in table 3.3, they write the misspelled word in the first box. In the second box, they try to spell the word correctly. The paper is passed to all the students in the group, and each attempts to write the correct spelling of the word. When the paper is returned to its owner, the students discuss how they think the word should be spelled and why. Answering "Because that's the way you spell it" is not acceptable. In this example, noting that the word *rest* is in the middle of *interesting* might help with its spelling.

| intresting | intersting | interesting | intresting |
| tipewriter | tipewriter | typeriter | typewriter |

Table 3.3

Modeling Whole Class Mini-Lessons

In this section of the chapter, two mini-lessons will be modeled. The purpose is to give you an idea of how you might go about presenting a mini-lesson to your class. Should you choose to try this mini-lesson, do not feel you have to use these exact words. Hopefully, this modeling will give you a general idea of what to say.

How to Have-a-Go-at-It

"Today I'd like to show you something you can do when you are not sure how to spell a word. It's called 'Have-a-go-at-it.' (Write this on the chalkboard.) When you have-a-go-at a word, you write it several different ways to see if one of those ways looks right to you. Let me show you a piece I've been working on. I made a transparency of it to give you an idea of how I've had-a-go-at a few words. Notice the word *accomodate*. I wasn't quite sure how to spell it, so I wrote it several different ways on the side of my paper. I decided that *accommodate* looked right, so I changed the spelling to a-c-c-o-m-m-o-d-a-t-e. When I first wrote it, I only had one *m*.

"Here's another word I had-a-go-at. I knew the word *seperate* didn't look right, so I wrote it several times on the side of my paper. *Separate* looked right, so I changed the spelling to s-e-p-a-r-a-t-e.

"Are there any examples you can share where you have used the have-a-go-at-it strategy? (Solicit responses from students and discuss).

"Today when you're writing and you know you haven't spelled a word right, try having a-go-at-it. You can use the side of your paper or a separate sheet of paper. It doesn't matter. When I confer with some of you today, be ready to show me if you had a go at it."

This mini-lesson included many of the characteristics of a good mini-lesson. It came from the needs of the students (all students can benefit from this strategy), it was short (only about five minutes), it taught one thing, it had a purpose (to help students with the confirming part of the spelling process), it added to class knowledge (not everyone will try this strategy today, but the information has been shared), a form of literature was used, and it ended with a connection ("Today when you're writing. . .").

Proofreading for Spelling

"Today I'd like to share with you a way to proofread your work for spelling. You would use this method when you have finished revising a piece of writing and want to do a final edit. I made a transparency of a story that a student wrote and I'm going to use it to show you how to proofread for spelling.

"When you proofread for spelling, you need to start at the end of your piece. The reason for this is that it's hard to catch spelling errors when you start at the beginning of your piece because you get caught up in the content. If you start at the end, you'll be able to focus on each word. So let's start at the end of this piece and circle words that are misspelled. Here's one, let's circle that. Here's another, so I'm going to circle it. (Continue until you have circled all the misspelled words in the piece with the students' input.)

"Today, if you're doing a final edit on a piece of writing, proofread for spelling like we've just done. Start at the end of the piece and work backwards. Circle any words you think are misspelled." (The next logical mini-lesson might be how to use sources to find the correct spelling of the misspelled words.)

Like the one above, this lesson has many of the characteristics of good mini-lessons. It comes from the needs of the students, is short, and has the purpose of helping students get better at finding misspelled words in their writing. This lesson taught one thing, added to the knowledge the class has about proofreading, and ended with a connection.

Keeping Track of Mini-Lessons

It is strongly suggested that you keep track of the mini-lessons you give. Note whether the mini-lesson was a whole class or small group lesson and the date it was given. You might consider making yourself a monthly calendar in which you can fill in the date of each mini-lesson. A simple list is also acceptable. This documentation serves as a record for you, parents, and administrators.

You might also start a file folder for each mini-lesson you give. In the folder, put any materials you used with the lesson and some notes about how your students received it. You won't be able to give the same mini-lessons with each class of students, but there are some mini-lessons that you will probably teach year after year. The folders come in handy for those kinds of lessons.

4

Spelling Mini-Lessons: Small Group Instruction

When teaching spelling through writing, instruction takes place in three settings: whole class mini-lessons, described in the previous chapter; small group mini-lessons; and during conferences with individual students. This chapter will focus on small group mini-lessons, discussing how they fit into the writing period and what role individual mini-lessons play.

Examples of Small Group Mini-Lessons

The topics of your small group mini-lessons will depend on the needs of your students. These lessons are taught to a small group of students who have demonstrated a particular spelling error pattern through their writing samples and daily written work. Mini-lessons take place about two days a week. The examples that follow are only that; they are not meant to determine your curriculum. *What you teach your students should be determined by their needs.*

Apostrophes in Contractions

A third-grader spelled *can't* as *ca'nt*. Another spelled *hasn't* as *hasnt*. Both of these students do not understand the meaning behind the apostrophe in contractions. A mini-lesson on this topic would show that apostrophes are placeholders for letters in contractions and that the apostrophes stand for certain letters.

One way to teach such a mini-lesson would be to make a list of contractions with the students' help. They can find examples in literature, select words posted around the room, or generate them from memory. After the words are listed, ask students what they notice about them. Help them discover a general principle that they can use in future writing. One class suggested that the apostrophe stands for a letter or letters and that in many cases the omitted letter is *o* (wouldn't, can't, didn't, haven't).

Apostrophes to Show Possession

Many upper-grade students experience problems using apostrophes to show possession. A mini-lesson on this topic would start with a list of words using apostrophes to show possession. These can be taken from literature or generated by you and your students. You might make a column with singular nouns and another with plural nouns, as in table 4.1. Ask the students to try and discover a pattern, helping them to see how ownership is conveyed.

Singular Noun	Singular Possessive	Plural Noun	Plural Possessive
girl	girl's	girls	girls'
dog	dog's	dogs	dogs'
street	street's	streets	streets'
child	child's	children	children's

Table 4.1.

Don't be surprised if your students begin to place an apostrophe before each s at the end of a word. Using apostrophes to show possession is a concept that must be taught again and again. Students also must understand the concept of plurals before they will be able to internalize the difference between a plural and a possessive.

Homophones

Students at all levels spell homophones incorrectly. This problem probably is related more to meaning than to spelling. Once students learn the meaning behind the words, they will begin to spell them correctly. Which spelling of *their, there,* or *they're* a student uses depends on the intended meaning.

A mini-lesson on this topic would list examples of homophones and discuss their meanings. Finding homophones in literature is helpful, because the words are in context. You might ask students to think as a whole class about the homophones they know and make a collective list of them. You can have the "homophones of the day" and write different homophones and their meanings. Ask students to orally create sentences using the words.

The *Reading Teacher's Book of Lists* (Fry et al., 1984) is an excellent source for finding lists of homophones, contractions, and so forth.

Doubling a Final Consonant Before Adding an Ending

Most of the time, before an ending such as *ing* or *ed* is added to a word the final consonant is doubled. One way to help students remember this generalization is to explain that the root, or base, word needs some kind of protection before the ending is added, so the last consonant is doubled. Words taken from literature are useful in pointing out this concept to students. Another way to help students understand this principle is to compile a list of words, each of which has the final consonant doubled before the ending is added. Ask the students what they notice about the list. Lead them to see that the word, which usually has a short vowel in it, needs to be protected from the ending, so its last consonant is doubled.

Capitalizing Proper Nouns

Helping students recognize that proper nouns are always capitalized is not difficult in a small group mini-lesson. Once again, using literature to provide examples is helpful. You might present different pages from a book and ask students to focus on the words that begin with capital letters. What kinds of words, aside from those at the beginning of a sentence, begin with capitals? Help them discover that names of people and places begin with capitals. It is not necessary to make lists of people and places to teach the concept of capitalizing proper nouns.

Correctly Spelling High Frequency Words

How do you know if a misspelled word is a high frequency word for a particular grade level? There are lists available, but as you examine your students' writing samples and written work, you will notice who misspells the basic high frequency words.

One way to help students with this concept in a small group mini-lesson is to tell them that words they use a lot in their writing are considered high frequency words and therefore their spellings have to be memorized. Give the students their original writing samples and 3-x-5-inch cards on which to write the high frequency words from those samples that cause them problems. They should also look through current pieces of writing for misspelled high frequency words. The students should tape these cards to the corner of their desks so they can refer to them frequently.

Making Plurals from Words Ending in *x, s, sh, ch*

Many spelling errors can be cleared up by teaching students that plurals for words ending in *x, s, sh,* and *ch* are formed by adding *es*. To teach this mini-lesson, make transparencies of several pages of a book you have recently read aloud to the class, one that has examples of plurals ending in *es*. Underline these words on the transparency. (Or you can generate a list of words that end with *x*, *s*, *sh*, or *ch* and are made into plurals by adding *es*.) First, talk about the concept of plurals. Then ask students what they notice about the way the plurals are formed. Help them to discover the generalization that *es* should be added to words ending in *x*, *s*, *sh*, or *ch* to make a plural.

Words Beginning with *kn* and *n*

Teaching the concept that words beginning with the sound of *n* may be written with *kn* is useful for both reading and spelling. You might make a list of words, all of which begin with the sound of *n*. Some of those words should start with *kn* and some should start with *n*. As you read them aloud, ask the students what they notice. Help them discover that sometimes words that begin with the sound of *n* are written with *kn*. They just have to memorize those words.

Encouraging students to be "word wizards" is a good way to help them see such patterns outside their usual reading and writing. For example, once you have taught this mini-lesson, award "word wizard" certificates to those who can find words that begin with *kn* in the print they encounter in their everyday lives. This type of activity helps students see that the concept you are teaching extends beyond the classroom.

The Two Sounds of *c*: *k* and *s*

Here is another example of a mini-lesson that is useful for reading as well as spelling. When teaching this concept, make a list of words that begin with *c*, or have the students find words from literature that begin with *c*. As you list and read them, ask the students what they notice about the sound made by the *c*. Help them to see that a *c* followed by an *e* or *i* usually has the sound of *s*, whereas a *c* followed by an *a*, *o*, or *u* usually has the sound of *k*.

By now, you have probably discovered the technique used in each of these mini-lessons: List words that contain a pattern you want the students to become familiar with, or find pages from literature that have examples of what you are trying to teach; have the students help you point out these patterns; and help them discover a generalization they can take with them to use in their writing.

Dropping the *e* Before Adding *ing*

This is a fairly easy concept to teach, but it does not appear to be an easy concept to learn because so many students forget to drop the *e* before adding the *ing*.

With this mini-lesson, begin by having the students help you generate a list of words, from memory or from literature, that end in *e*. Start the list with words such as *hope, rake, bake,* and so forth. Ask the students what they notice about these words (long vowel sound, word ends in *e*, and so on). Rewrite each word with an *-ing* ending. Ask if they noticed what you did when you added *-ing* to ecah word. Help them see that when a word with a long vowel sound ends in *e*, the *e* is usually dropped before *ing* is added. Next, have students predict the spelling of words by applying the generalization they have just learned. For example, ask them to predict the spelling of *taking* by looking at *take*, the spelling of *replacing* by looking at *replace*, and the spelling of *hoping* by looking at *hope*. It's a good idea to add some words to the list that do not fit the pattern. For example, the word *have* does not contain a long vowel sound, but the *e* is dropped before adding *ing*.

Modeling Small Group Mini-Lessons

This section will model two of the small group mini-lesson listed above. Once again, the purpose is not to put words in your mouth, but merely to help you see how you might present your own mini-lesson.

Correctly Spelling High Frequency Words

Start the mini-lesson by giving students their writing samples. (It is helpful to make copies of the writing samples before you start to analyze them so you can use them in mini-lessons.) Say, "As I looked over your writing samples, I noticed that you are misspelling what are called high frequency words. These are words that you see over and over again in books, and words that you use a lot in your own writing. These words are the ones you just have to memorize because you use them a lot when you write.

"I have made some transparencies of pages from a book. Let's see if we can figure out which of these words would be called high frequency words and circle those. (Proceed to circle the high frequency words with the help of the students.)

"Now, look over your writing sample and see if you can find high frequency words you misspelled. Circle these. You don't have to circle all the misspelled words, just those that you think are high frequency words—those that you see all the time in books and use in your own writing.

"I'm going to give each of you a 3-x-5 card. What I'd like you to do is write the correct spelling of these words on the card. Then you can tape the card to the top part of your desk so you can see the correct spelling of these words each time you write." At this point you may have to help the students as they go through their writing samples to select the high frequency words. They should also add high frequency words from current writing to the card.

Dropping the e Before Adding ing

To begin the mini-lesson, gather the students who in their writing samples and daily written work have failed to follow this spelling principle. Begin with, "Let's make a list of words that end in *e*, because I want to show you something about them. I've started the list with a few words. I've got *make, save, notice,* and *reduce.* What other words can you add? Some of you can look in a book you are now reading to see if you can find examples of words that end in *e*."

After you have a list of ten to twelve words, ask, "What do you notice about these words?" (Help the students see that most of the words end in *e* and have a long vowel sound.) Now rewrite each word by dropping the *e* and adding *ing*. Continue with, "What should you do if you want to add *ing* to these words? That's right, the *e* should be dropped before you add *ing* because when a word has a long vowel sound and ends in *e*, we usually drop the *e* before adding *ing*.

"I've noticed in your writing that when you are spelling words that end in *e* and have a long vowel sound, you are forgetting to drop the *e* before adding the *ing*. That's a spelling generalization that holds true most of the time: When a word with a long vowel sound ends in *e*, drop the *e* before adding the *ing*."

End the mini-lesson with, "When you're writing in school and at home, see if you can remember to drop the *e* before adding *ing*. Let me know when you catch yourself doing this."

Fitting Small Group Mini-Lessons into the Writing Period

Small group mini-lessons can be integrated into the regular writing routine in a variety of ways. One teacher started the writing period with a whole class procedural writing mini-lesson explaining where to put final edited drafts. After the students started to work on their writing, he called a small group of students together for a spelling mini-lesson. They gathered on the floor around the teacher, who proceeded to talk to them about the use of apostrophes for possessions. After the mini-lesson, the students returned to their desks and worked on their writing while he conferred individually with several children, only one of whom was in the apostrophe small group. The writing period ended in an author's chair (in which students share and get feedback on their writing).

Another teacher started the writing period simply by asking the students to begin writing. She then convened a small group for a spelling mini-lesson on homonyms. After the mini-lesson, the students went back and joined their classmates, who were still writing. The teacher walked around and conferred with students, some of whom were at the mini-lesson and some who were not. The writing period ended with an author's chair, just as all writing periods in her class end. One student from the small group talked about how he had changed the spelling of homonyms in his paper after his mini-lesson. Other students asked for feedback about the content of their pieces.

Individual Mini-Lessons

As you confer individually with students about their writing, there will be times when you want to talk with them about their spelling. You might want to give reminders and check to see if they are

- circling words they think are misspelled;
- keeping up with their spelling logs;
- implementing what you have taught in whole class and small group mini-lessons;
- exhibiting evidence of having-a-go-at-it

You also can ask the students to show you a word they know is misspelled. Write the standard spelling of the word over the student's incorrect spelling and point out any similarities and differences. For example, if a student spells *tomorrow* as *tomarow*, point out that the student has correctly spelled the beginning and end of the word and show how the middle of the word is different. Ask the student to think of a way to remember the correct spelling of that part of the word. This word can be added to the spelling log.

Teachers sometimes ask how often they should plan on having spelling conferences. It is a difficult question to answer—some students will need these more than others. When you confer with students, only part of the discussion should be concerned with spelling; otherwise, students will quickly get the idea that spelling is the most important thing about writing. If you confer with each student at least once a week during writing, spelling should be a part of those conferences on a regular basis.

5

Assessment in a Program that Teaches Spelling Through Writing

When evaluating students' work in a spelling through writing program, teachers must take a different approach than they would take in a traditional spelling program. There are several pieces to consider: your assessment of student progress; your assessment of student attitudes; and student assessment of their progress and attitudes.

Teacher Assessment of Student Progress

Teachers who teach spelling through writing usually have to give a letter grade for spelling on a report card. How can such a grade be determined? There are numerous ways to go about deciding upon a grade, including

- asking students to write and turn in an edited final draft to be graded for spelling;

- looking at checklists and anecdotal records collected from spelling conferences and observations; and

- assessing progress toward spelling goals.

Edited Drafts

You can ask for these drafts on a monthly or quarterly basis. Students can choose a piece they like and proofread it for spelling, using the procedure outlined in a mini-lesson in chapter 3. You can derive a spelling grade by calculating the percentage of words spelled correctly; you may want to factor in the number of words that were circled because the student knew they were misspelled. In this way you can come up with a figure that can be translated into a grade.

You can also use the same writing sample to look at students' progress in revision and general editing. If you choose this route, require that all drafts be turned in with revisions shown, and ask students to staple an editing checklist to their paper. This editing checklist is a list of things you want students to look for as they edit. A second-grade checklist might include

- name and date on paper
- end marks
- capital letters at the beginning of sentences
- capital letters at the beginning of names, and
- circling misspelled words.

A fifth-grade checklist might include

- end marks
- capital letters at the beginning of sentences and for proper nouns
- commas
- correct use of quotation marks
- use of apostrophe to show possession, and
- circling misspelled words.

What you put on the list depends on you and the individual and group needs of your students. Some students may be required to edit for each thing on the list, while others may only be asked to look for three or four items.

Checklists and Anecdotal Records

Checklists can be made up to reflect whatever you feel is important about spelling. As you confer with and observe students, you can complete these checklists before a grading period and use the information to help determine a grade. *Spelling in Whole Language Classrooms* (Buchanan, 1989) has a list of spelling behaviors you might want to observe, such as

- willingness to take risks
- interest in spelling

- use of resources
- willingness to do quick checks and edit, and
- ability to identify misspellings.

Each of these can be marked with "demonstrates consistently," "demonstrates some of the time," or "working on" to indicate students' progress.

Figure 5.1 (page 45) shows how one fourth-grade teacher put together these behaviors on a checklist. Each behavior is given a + if it is demonstrated consistently, a ✓ if the student demonstrates it some of the time, and a / if the student is working on the behavior. As the time for grades approaches, the teacher fills out the checklist based on her observations and anecdotal records. If she cannot evaluate a particular behavior for a child, she makes it a point to observe that child during the next week.

How will you know if a child exhibits a certain behavior? Here are some examples that might help. The teacher mentioned above knew that a girl named Julie was using sources when she was trying to spell the word "excalibur" in her story. She and her family had been to Las Vegas and had stayed at the Excalibur Hotel. They brought back a souvenir ashtray with the word printed on it, so she copied down the word at home and brought it to school so she could spell it correctly in her story.

In another case, the teacher noticed during a conference that Jeff had circled the word *crep* and had written *creep* above it. When asked where he found the correct spelling, he said his parents don't like to fight in front of the kids, so they write notes to each other. He had read one of the notes and had seen the word *creep* and remembered how to spell it. Both of these students were demonstrating that they used resources to help with spelling.

This checklist can be made into an insert for the report card. The teacher who used this list as an insert found that parents appreciated the additional, and more useful, information about their students' spelling achievement.

Progress Toward Goals

An excellent whole class mini-lesson is to ask students what strategies good spellers use to find the correct spelling of a word and what they personally would like to do better as spellers. Write these responses down as they are made. Then ask students to choose at least one of these as a goal. You should choose an additional one for each student so that everyone has two goals for that grading period. (For second-graders, you might want to start with just one goal that student and teacher have agreed upon.)

—Text continues on page 46

Teacher Assessment of Student Progress / 45

Name	Willingness to risk	Interest in spelling	Uses resources	Willingness to do quick checks and edit	Ability to identify misspellings

+ = demonstrates consistently
✓ = demonstrates some of the time
/ = working on

Fig. 5.1. Teacher Observations of Student Progress in Spelling

The list of strategies for finding the spelling of unknown words could be goals. These include:

- look in your reading book;
- look in the atlas;
- look in the name book if you're looking for a name;
- look around the room for the word;
- look on the 100-most-frequent-words list;
- ask someone;
- sound it out;
- write it, and see if it looks right;
- look up the word in the dictionary;
- have a go at it;
- see if you can find it in the newspaper.

Routman (1991) compiled a list of additional items that may be of use as goals.

- keep the spelling log up to date;
- be ready for a spelling conference;
- circle misspelled words when editing;
- spell words correctly that you know how to spell;
- use the have-a-go-at-it strategy more;
- take a risk to use words not usually used in writing;
- ask if a word looks right if you think it's spelled incorrectly.

Before the grading period, confer with each student, asking for evidence of progress toward goals. For example, evidence of having used an atlas would involve showing in the atlas where the student looked up a word needed during writing and correctly spelled it. Evidence of having used the have-a-go-at-it strategy would be to show an instance where the strategy was used on the side of the paper or on a separate sheet of paper.

Parents are especially interested in spelling goals and the progress their children are making, so sharing them at parent conferences is helpful.

Teacher Assessment of Attitudes

One way to assess students' attitudes about spelling is to administer an interview at the beginning and end of the school year. Buchanan (1989) and Routman (1991) propose numerous questions you can ask. The form shown in figure 5.2 (page 48) was adapted from suggestions in *Spelling for Whole Language Classrooms* (Buchanan, 1989).

Answers on the interview can be coded according to the type of answer given by the child. For example, the reply to the first question, "What is spelling?" can be coded as a phonics-based answer (spelling is sounding out words), a meaning-based answer (spelling is something that allows others to read your work), or an object-based answer (spelling is a test, a list of words). An answer to question 4(b) in the figure can be coded as to whether the student has-a-go-at-it, asks someone, or uses one of the sources in the room.

The purpose of coding answers is to give you a sense of how your students' attitudes toward spelling have changed over the school year. For example, you can figure out the percentage of students who gave a phonics-based answer to question 1 at the beginning of the year and compare it with the percent of phonics-based answers at the end of the year. When this interview was used by one teacher who was teaching spelling through writing, the answers at the beginning of the year to the first question were mostly phonics-based; students said that spelling was sounding out words. At the end of the year, most of the students gave a meaning-based answer to the same question; they thought spelling was something that was important in written work, especially in a final copy.

The beginning- and end-of-year answers to question 7 will also give you some insight into your students' attitudes about spelling. One teacher found that at the beginning of the year, most of her students thought a good speller was someone who got 100 percent on weekly tests. By the end of the year, most felt that a good speller was someone who read a lot and whose final drafts contained few misspelled words.

In this same classroom, students at the beginning of the year who felt they were good spellers thought so because they scored 100 percent on spelling tests in previous classrooms. Those who didn't feel they were good spellers thought so because they didn't get 100 percent. At the end of the year, almost all students who felt they were good spellers thought so because they read a lot and tried to spell words correctly in their final drafts. They also felt they were good spellers because they knew what to do when they couldn't spell a word: have-a-go-at-it, use sources in the room (atlas, newspaper, books, dictionary, etc.), or ask someone.

Name_____

Date_____

1. What is spelling?

2. How do you think you learned to spell?

3. Should you always spell every word correctly in your writing? Why or why not?

4. What do you do when you don't know how to spell a word:
   a)   in rough draft?

   b)   in final draft?

5. Do you have any tricks you use to help you remember how to spell some words?

6. What would you like to do to get better as a speller?

7. Who's a good speller that you know? What makes him/her a good speller?

8. Do you think you are a good speller? Why or why not?

Adapted from *Spelling for Whole Language Classrooms*, Ethel Buchanan.

Fig. 5.2. Spelling Interview

It has been mentioned that the interview should be given at the beginning and end of the school year. However, you should feel free to conduct the interview at any time. Some teachers like to give it at the beginning, middle, and end of the year in order to determine instructional needs and find out if students' views are changing.

Student Assessment of Progress and Attitudes

Students are very capable of assessing their own progress in, and attitudes about, spelling by using a spelling evaluation sheet, looking at spelling growth in written work, and gauging progress toward goals.

Spelling Evaluation Sheets

A week or two before grades are due, give each student a self-evaluation sheet. The one shown in figure 5.3 was adapted from information in *Write On* (Parry and Hornsby, 1988).

Name_____ Date_____

Grade_____

	Yes	Sometimes	No
1. I care about spelling.			
2. I write often.			
3. I proofread my writing.			
4. I read every day.			
5. I explore words.			
6. I check to be sure.			
7. I learn new spellings.			

Comments

Fig. 5.3. Spelling Evaluation

Reprinted by permission of Jo-Ann Parry and David Hornsby: *Write On: A Conference Approach to Writing.* (Heinemann, a division of Reed Publishing (USA), Inc., Portsmouth, NH, 1985).

When using an evaluation such as this one, you have to explain to students what is meant by "I care about spelling," "I explore words," and so on. A good mini-lesson is to ask them to brainstorm about what they think is meant by these terms and use their answers as the basis for evaluation.

This activity can be done as a class if you make a transparency of the form and walk students through it as they have their copies in front of them. You will also need to model what you would like them to put in the "comments" section of the evaluation. Included here are a couple of samples from students in second and fourth grades (figures 5.4 and 5.5—on page 51).

Name CONOR   Date 12-15-92
Grade 2

	Yes	Sometimes	No
1. I care about spelling.		✓	
2. I write often.	✓		
3. I proofread my writing.	✓		
4. I read every day.		✓	
5. I explore words	✓		
6. I check to be sure.		✓	
7. I learn new spellings.	✓		

Comments I care about spelling when it's a big proget

Fig. 5.4. Spelling Evaluation

Something you might consider adding to the bottom of the sheet is a place where students can put what they think their grade should be for that grading period and why.

Student Assessment of Progress and Attitudes / 51

Name **Brendan**   Date **5/15/91**
Grade **4th**

	Yes	Sometimes	No
1. I care about spelling.		✓	
2. I write often.	✓		
3. I proofread my writing.		✓	
4. I read every day.	✓		
5. I explore words.		✓	
6. I check to be sure.	✓		
7. I learn new spellings.	✓		

Comments *Because I think I'm a fairly good speller because I can spell a lot of common words right. I think I need to work on proof-reading final drafts*

Fig. 5.5. Spelling Evaluation

Looking at Written Work

Another way to help students assess themselves as spellers is to have them look at their pieces of writing for evidence of progress in spelling. As they examine their drafts, they will begin to discover that they now spell words correctly that they used to misspell. You can ask them to list such words as a measurement of their growth.

Progress Toward Goals

Spelling goals were brought up earlier in this chapter. In that section it was mentioned that after a list of goals has been developed, the teacher and student can choose a goal (or goals) for that student during a brief conference. Students can assess their progress by demonstrating how well they have achieved those goals.

Assessment is not difficult in teaching spelling through writing if you, the students, and their parents know what the students will be assessed on. The important thing is to decide upon the criteria and make sure everyone knows them.

6

Lingering Questions

The purpose of this final chapter is to address some questions that may not have been answered for you so far. These questions are regularly asked by teachers who are teaching spelling through writing or who want to do so.

1. How do I explain this kind of program to parents, especially those who want spelling lists?

Parents are reluctant to give up the notion of spelling tests, probably because they are familiar with them from their own schooling (Routman, 1991). The ritual of helping a child study for the weekly spelling test is something concrete parents can do, and it gives them a sense of helping with their child's learning.

Parents are most fearful when they don't understand something. At a back-to-school-night program or parent night, explain why and how you are teaching spelling through writing. Show the initial writing samples and the steps you have gone through to determine individual spelling needs. Assure parents that spelling instruction will take place, but in a different way than they—and their child—might be used to. Model a mini-lesson that you might give to the whole class and to a small group. Explain how you will assess their children's progress in spelling, and challenge them to help by encouraging their children to become word wizards. Explain the system you use to have your students proofread for spelling and how important it is to spell correctly in final drafts. Show examples of how we all use functional spelling now and then. If parents are unable to attend the meeting, be ready to put the information you wish to convey into a letter. Gentry (1987) and Wilde (1992) give examples of letters you can send home to parents.

Invite parents to visit during spelling mini-lessons and to follow you around as you hold spelling conferences. Show results of the spelling interviews. Keep the first writing sample and have parents compare it with a writing sample at midyear and the end of the year. When parents see how their children's spelling improves in writing, they will become supporters of your program.

2. Are there any other activities I can use that will help my students with spelling?

In addition to the lessons mentioned earlier in this text, there are numerous activities you can engage your students in to help them with spelling. The daily edit, wall charts, personal dictionary, and categorization games are but a few.

To do a daily edit (Buchanan, 1989), type a paragraph from a book, making numerous errors in spelling and punctuation. Make a copy for each student in the class or write it on the chalkboard. The assignment is to find as many spelling and punctuation errors as possible. After working individually, the students should work together in small groups of three or four to compare answers. As a large group, go over the paragraph, pointing out correct spelling and punctuation. This exercise will help students with their own proofreading work.

The personal dictionary can take many forms. Routman (1991) explains how words learned through the have-a-go-at-it sheet can be written on 3-x-5-inch cards and placed alphabetically in a file box. You might also staple pages together in a booklet, one page for each letter of the alphabet. As students learn how to spell words, they can record them in the book.

These words should be thought of as words that should rarely be misspelled. Get the students into the habit of looking in their personal dictionaries when they are unsure of the spelling of a word and when they are proofreading.

Wall charts (Parry and Hornsby, 1988; Routman, 1991) are places to display words that students may need in their spelling. Words can be grouped around a theme (holidays, seasons, numbers, verbs, other words such as *said*, etc.) or a pattern (*ing* words, contractions, words with a particular prefix or suffix, etc.). These patterns can come from words generated in mini-lessons or from reading assignments. You may be the one to start the charts, but students should be free to add words when they find examples in their reading and writing.

Categorization activities are a great way to lead students to focus on patterns and features of words. Words can come from spelling logs, the snare board, content areas, etc. Ask students to work in pairs or triads to decide what words could go together and why. Each group can share their work with the whole class.

There are a few commercial spelling games that are helpful, such as Spill n' Spell and Scrabble Junior. Any games that help students focus on patterns in words are useful.

3. How will my students do on the spelling subtests of standardized tests?

No one really knows how they will do. In a study mentioned earlier in this text, students who were taught spelling through writing and students who used a traditional text were given the spelling subtest of a standardized test at the beginning and end of the school year. Neither group showed a *significant* gain from the first to the second test, although both groups showed a slight increase.

The spelling subtest of most standardized tests is actually a proofreading test rather than a spelling test. To really test spelling, students should be asked to write out the word. An interesting research study, one that you might do as a teacher researcher, is to see if the test scores increase by focusing on proofreading skills.

Test scores are important to parents, teachers, and administrators. If you are teaching spelling through writing and must give the spelling subtest of a standardized test, it's important to collect additional data that show student achievement. One way is to collect writing samples and compare the ratio of the number of words written to the number of words correctly spelled. Another is to look at students' changes in attitudes and strategies through a spelling interview.

4. Is this way to teach spelling a lot more work than using a spelling list or spelling book?

At first, yes, just as any new way of teaching may create more work initially. You'll find that it takes a while to analyze the writing samples and complete the spelling evaluation sheets for each student. Soon, however, you'll be able to look at a set of writing samples and quickly jot down the patterns of spelling errors that you notice and the names of the students who need help in each category.

5. What should I do if my administrator doesn't support me in my attempts to teach spelling through writing?

Keeping your administrator informed is one way to gain support. Be sure to give notice of any changes you would like to make in your spelling program (Routman, 1991). Invite your administrator into your classroom to see how you give a mini-lesson, how the children use have-a-go sheets, how students write words in their personal dictionaries, and how they use sources to find unknown words. Share books and articles that will help your administrator understand the philosophy of teaching spelling through writing. Make sure it is clear you are not neglecting the teaching of spelling, merely going about it in another way.

You may have an administrator who insists that you use a list. If so, ask students to find words from their writing that they know are misspelled. These words can become the words on their own personal lists, which they can administer to each other. Continue to give spelling mini-lessons and try some of the other activities described in this text.

6. How can I convince other teachers to use this kind of program?

You can't. A teacher who has to be convinced to implement something probably isn't ready for it. Think about yourself: You probably try something new as a teacher because you want to. You've probably read something or heard something that leads you to believe that you would like to change what you are doing.
If other teachers express interest in how you are teaching spelling through writing, willingly share with them. Invite them in to see your mini-lessons and show them how you analyze writing samples. Collect informal data that will show that your program is working, and share this information with them.

7. What about spelling bees?

Who are spelling bees for? They're for good spellers—to show the others what they know. The students who need more practice in spelling are the ones who miss first and end up sitting at their desks while the good spellers continue. Spelling bees really don't help anyone. If your school district has a district-wide spelling bee and students want to participate, help them learn how to study the words at home. Students who spell well enough to go to district-wide spelling bees are usually motivated to study on their own.

And in Conclusion...

The purpose of this book has been to help teachers learn how to teach spelling through writing. Reasons you might want to teach spelling through writing were outlined, and forming groups was discussed. Numerous large and small group mini-lessons were presented. Evaluation was discussed and some lingering questions were answered.
Spelling should be fun—for you and for your students. It should be something that students are interested in and motivated to learn. Hopefully, the ideas presented in this book will help as you move toward teaching spelling through writing.

References

Atwell, Nancie. *In the Middle*. Portsmouth, NH: Heinemann, 1987.

Bean, Wendy, and C. Bouffler. *Spell by Writing*. Portsmouth, NH: Heinemann, 1987.

Buchanan, Ethyl. *Spelling for Whole Language Classrooms*. Katonah, NY: Richard C. Owens, 1989.

Calkins, Lucy. *The Art of Teaching Writing*. Portsmouth, NH: Heinemann, 1986.

Crafton, Linda. *Whole Language: Getting Started. . .Moving Forward*. Katonah, NY: Richard C. Owens, 1991.

Cochrane, Orin, et al. *Reading, Writing and Caring*. Katonah, NY: Richard C. Owens, 1984.

Fry, Edward B., et al. *Reading Teacher's Book of Lists*. Englewood Cliffs, NJ: Prentice-Hall, 1984.

Gentry, Richard. *Spel. . .Is a Four Letter Word*. Portsmouth, NH: Heinemann, 1987.

———. "An Analysis of Developmental Spelling in GYNS AT WORK." *The Reading Teacher* (November 1982): 192–200.

Goodman, Yetta, and C. Burke. *Reading Strategies: Focus on Comprehension*. New York: Holt, 1980.

Hagerty, Patricia. *Readers' Workshop: Real Reading*. Ontario, Canada: Scholastic, 1992.

Hagerty, Patricia, and J. Partridge. "Learning to Spell Through Writing: A Case Study." Paper presented at the 41st Annual Meeting of the National Reading Conference, December 1991, Palm Springs, CA.

Hornsby, David, et al. *Read On: A Conference Approach to Reading*. Portsmouth, NH: Heinemann, 1986.

Nathan, Ruth, et al. *Classroom Strategies That Work*. Portsmouth, NH: Heinemann, 1989.

Parry, Jo-Ann, and D. Hornsby. *Write On: A Conference Approach to Writing*. 1st U.S. ed. Portsmouth, NH: Heinemann, 1988.

Routman, Regie. *Invitations*. Portsmouth, NH: Heinemann, 1991.

Sitton, Rebecca, and R. Forest. *The Quick-Word Handbook for Everyday Writers*. North Billerica, MA: Curriculum Associates, 1987.

Wilde, Sandra. "A Proposal for a New Spelling Curriculum." *The Elementary School Journal*. (January 1990): 275–289.

Wilde, Sandra. *You Kan Red This!* Portsmouth, NH: Heinemann, 1992.

About the Author

Pat Hagerty is currently an associate professor in the Division of Elementary, Middle School, Early Childhood, and Reading at the University of Northern Colorado. She teaches reading and language arts methods courses as well as courses in the master's and doctoral programs. She is a consultant to many schools and school districts on topics such as Whole Language Instruction, Readers' Workshop, Writers' Workshop, and spelling instruction. She is the author of *Readers' Workshop: Real Reading*, published by Scholastic (1992).

/372.632H144T>C1/